The Art of Real Estate

John Graff

Ellimat Books

Copyright © 2023 by Ellimat Books

All rights reserved. No part of this publication may be reproduced, distributed, or transmitted in any form or by any means, including photocopying, recording, or other electronic or mechanical methods, without the prior written permission of the publisher, except in the case of brief quotations embodied in critical reviews and certain other noncommercial uses permitted by copyright law.

ISBN: 979-8-9895666-1-7 (paperback)

Although the advice and information in this book are believed to be accurate and true as of the time of publication, neither the authors nor the publisher can accept any legal responsibility or liability for any inaccuracies or any loss, harm, or injury that comes about from following instructions or advice in the book.

First Edition published by Ellimat Books 2023

Contents

1. Introduction — 1
2. Laying The Plans — 5
3. Waging War — 14
4. Attack By Strategy — 22
5. Tactical Dispositions — 30
6. Energy — 37
7. Weak Points and Strong — 44
8. Maneuvering — 53
9. Variation of Tactics — 63
10. The Army On The March — 68
11. Terrain — 78
12. The Nine Situations — 90

13. The Attack By Fire   100

14. The Use of Spies   104

Chapter 1

Introduction

Sun Tzu's "The Art of War" is a timeless masterpiece that has transcended generations, offering profound insights into strategy, leadership, and the pursuit of victory. Its wisdom has influenced military commanders, business leaders, and thinkers throughout history. But what if we could apply this ancient wisdom to a modern field, one that constantly demands adaptability, strategy, and resilience? In "The Art of Real Estate," that is precisely what the author sets out to achieve.

The real estate industry is a battlefield of its own, where agents are warriors engaged in a ceaseless struggle for success. The competitive nature of this field, characterized by shifting market dynamics, intricate negotiations, and the pursuit of strategic advantage, closely mirrors the principles laid out by Sun Tzu centuries ago.

In this unique adaptation of "The Art of War," the author takes Sun Tzu's teachings and translates them into actionable strategies for real estate professionals. By drawing parallels between the military and real estate worlds, they invite readers to explore how the principles of Sun Tzu can be leveraged to achieve triumph in the realm of property, transactions, and client relationships.

This book invites you to embark on a journey where battlefield tactics become tools of the trade, where the art of negotiation becomes a cornerstone of your success, and where strategic positioning and adaptability are your guiding stars. You will discover how intelligence gathering, resource optimization, and the mastery of conflict resolution can elevate your real estate career to new heights.

Through "The Art of Real Estate," the author hopes to offer a fresh perspective to both seasoned real estate agents and those new to the field. By marrying ancient wisdom with contemporary challenges, this book aims to provide you with a comprehensive toolkit for navigating the multifaceted landscape of real estate.

As you read through these pages, you will see how the author expertly aligns Sun Tzu's enduring principles with the intricacies of real estate, emphasizing that success in this field requires more than mere brute force. It requires strategy, adaptability, and the ability to see the bigger picture.

Whether you're a real estate veteran looking to sharpen your skills or a newcomer seeking guidance on your path to success, "The Art of War: Real Estate Edition" promises to be a valuable companion. It is a testament to the enduring relevance of ancient wisdom and its capacity to transform our approach to contemporary challenges.

JOHN GRAFF

Prepare to embark on a journey of strategic enlightenment, armed with the wisdom of Sun Tzu and guided by the insights of this book. We invite you to embrace the lessons within and become a real estate warrior who not only survives but thrives in this competitive arena. May your real estate endeavors be marked by triumph, resilience, and a profound understanding of the art of real estate, as inspired by "The Art of War."

Welcome to the intersection of ancient wisdom and modern success. The battle begins here.

Chapter 2

Laying The Plans

- Every real estate deal can be a significant financial decision for clients, affecting their lives and financial well-being. Therefore, understanding the intricacies of the market and negotiation is crucial.

- Successful real estate agents consider five constant factors when evaluating property transactions:

- The Moral Law represents ethical conduct and trustworthiness, which help agents build strong relationships with clients.

- Heaven signifies factors like market trends, interest rates, and economic conditions.

- Earth encompasses property location, condition, and market competition.

- The Commander symbolizes the real estate agent, embodying qualities like wisdom, sincerity, benevolence, courage, and strictness.

- Method and discipline involve organizing the process, maintaining professional standards, and managing resources efficiently.

- Real estate agents who adhere to ethical principles and prioritize their clients' best interests earn trust and loyalty, even in challenging transactions.

- Understanding the cyclical nature of the real estate market, seasonal fluctuations, and local climate can impact property value and buying decisions.

- In real estate, agents assess property location, neighborhood safety, accessibility, and property-specific risks, which influence property values and client choices.

- Real estate agents should possess qualities such as market knowledge, honesty, empathy, determination, and professionalism to lead their clients effectively.

- In real estate, this translates to organizing tasks efficiently, defining roles within a real estate team, managing resources effectively, and adhering to a budget.

- In real estate, agents who understand and master these five factors are more likely to succeed, while those who neglect them may struggle.

- In real estate, when analyzing property transactions, agents should consider these factors as a foundation for evaluating market conditions and client needs.

- When competing in the real estate market, agents should ask similar questions about themselves and their competitors to determine their strengths and weaknesses.

- Assessing these seven considerations can help real estate agents predict the success or challenges of a particular property transaction.

- In real estate, agents who follow effective strategies and advice are more likely to succeed, while those who ignore it may face difficulties.

- In real estate, agents should remain adaptable and open to seizing opportunities that may not fit traditional strategies.

- In real estate, flexibility and the ability to

adapt to changing market conditions are crucial for success.

- In real estate negotiations, some degree of strategic deception or negotiation tactics may be employed to achieve favorable outcomes.

- In real estate negotiations, the ability to control information and perceptions can be a valuable tool to secure favorable terms.

- In real estate, agents may use incentives or marketing strategies to attract potential buyers or sellers, creating a competitive advantage.

- In real estate, agents should strategize and

adapt to competitive scenarios, either by preparing for strong competitors or seeking alternative opportunities.

- In real estate negotiations, understanding the temperament and preferences of the other party can help agents tailor their approach for a more favorable outcome.

- In real estate, seizing opportunities to negotiate or acting swiftly when the other party is complacent can be advantageous.

- In real estate, agents may find success by targeting overlooked properties or entering unexpected markets.

- In real estate, successful strategies and tactics should be kept confidential to maintain a competitive edge.

In the realm of real estate, just as in the art of warfare, the victorious agent is akin to a seasoned general who meticulously calculates every move before stepping onto the battlefield. Before the ink dries on the contract, this astute agent has already made myriad calculations in their metaphorical temple. They have scrutinized property valuations, market trends, and client needs with the precision of an ancient scholar contemplating celestial patterns.

Conversely, the agent who faces defeat is often one who hastily engages without due forethought. They enter the fray with but a handful of calculations, blind to the intricate web of factors that govern real estate transactions. This lack of preparation often leads to their downfall.

Indeed, it is the multitude of calculations that pave the path to victory, for in these meticulous deliberations lies the wisdom to navigate the labyrinthine complexities of real estate. The agent who leaves no stone unturned, who contemplates every angle and scenario, emerges as the victor.

However, the gravest error lies in the absence of calculation altogether. To embark on a real estate endeavor without strategic forethought is akin to sailing into a tempest without a compass. Such recklessness often seals one's fate in the annals of defeat.

It is through a keen and unwavering focus on this principle that the discerning agent can predict with clarity who is destined for victory and who is poised for defeat in the ever-shifting landscape of real estate.

Chapter 3

Waging War

In the realm of real estate, much like in the operations of war, careful planning and resource management are essential to achieve success.

- In the world of real estate, consider a scenario where there are a thousand potential property deals, both swift and substantial, and a hundred thousand prospective clients, all requiring various services and resources. The expenses incurred, including marketing, client meetings, office supplies, and maintenance, can quickly accumulate, amounting to a significant financial outlay.

- When you engage in the actual process of buying or selling properties, delays in achieving success can lead to diminishing enthusiasm and reduced efficiency. Just as in war, if a deal takes too long to materialize, the excitement and energy of the parties involved may wane. Additionally, if you linger too long in negotiations or fail to make decisions promptly, your competitive advantage may dissipate.

- Prolonged real estate transactions can strain your financial resources and limit your ability to take advantage of other opportunities. The financial resources required for lengthy negotiations and protracted deals may exceed your initial estimates, leaving you financially stretched.

- Moreover, if your resources become depleted and your momentum wanes, you may find yourself vulnerable to competitors who are ready to seize opportunities in your stead. When your financial reserves are exhausted, it becomes challenging to fend off rival agents and agencies, regardless of your strategic acumen.

- It is important to recognize that while haste in real estate transactions can lead to poor decisions, excessive delays are rarely associated with favorable outcomes. A balance between swiftness and prudence is essential.

- In the world of real estate, there is no evidence to suggest that protracted negotiations or overly lengthy transactions benefit anyone involved. Prolonged waiting and indecision rarely yield better results.

- Only those who truly understand the negative consequences of prolonged real estate dealings can grasp the importance of conducting transactions efficiently and effectively.

- A skilled real estate agent minimizes the need for secondary efforts and does not burden themselves with excessive administrative tasks. Resources, both human and financial, should be deployed wisely.

- While it is advisable to bring necessary resources and materials from your office or home, such as market research and documents, it is often more efficient to source other required items, like property information, from the client or the property itself.

- Relying on external contributions to sustain your real estate activities can strain both the state of your finances and the goodwill of those you rely on for support.

- Conversely, the presence of an active real estate market in close proximity can lead to increased property values and, subsequently, higher costs for clients. This inflation can have a significant impact on the financial well-being of individuals and communities.

- When the cost of living rises due to inflated property prices, it places additional financial burdens on the general population, especially the working class.

- The consequences of these financial strains include a reduction in disposable income, which affects the livelihoods of ordinary people. Government expenses related to real estate, including taxes, permits, and infrastructure development, can also impose a significant financial burden.

- In real estate, as in war, it is often more advantageous to rely on the resources of others, such as clients or counterparties, to minimize the strain on your own resources. A small contribution from the other party can have a significant impact on the outcome of a transaction.

- To achieve success in real estate, it is important to keep your clients motivated and engaged. Rewards and incentives can be powerful tools to maintain enthusiasm and secure favorable outcomes in negotiations.

- When multiple parties are involved in a real estate transaction, the agent should recognize the contributions of those who made the initial efforts. This recognition can foster cooperation and unity among all parties involved.

- In real estate, using the expertise and resources of others, such as experienced professionals or counterparties, can enhance your capabilities and expand your reach.

- The primary objective in real estate, as in war, should be to achieve victory or success quickly, rather than engaging in lengthy campaigns or negotiations.

- In the world of real estate, the agent holds a significant role as the arbiter of clients' property-related fates. The agent's decisions and actions can determine whether clients experience successful transactions or face challenges in their real estate endeavors.

Chapter 4

Attack By Strategy

- In the realm of real estate, as in the art of war, the ultimate goal is not to destroy the market or the competition but to conquer and capture opportunities whole and intact. It is far more advantageous to secure a property deal in its entirety, including all its potential benefits, than to engage in a destructive rivalry.

- Thus, in the real estate arena, the paramount achievement is not merely to defeat competitors and demolish their efforts. Instead, it is to outmaneuver them strategically, securing opportunities without engaging in fierce battles.

- True excellence in real estate lies not in winning every skirmish but in adeptly overcoming obstacles without resorting to direct conflict.

- The highest form of real estate expertise is the ability to thwart the competition's plans, followed by preventing their consolidation of resources. Subsequently, one should aim to excel in the competitive field of property transactions. Engaging in lengthy and resource-draining property disputes, such as besieging deals or pursuing unproductive ventures, should be avoided whenever possible.

- It is a fundamental rule in real estate that besieging or pursuing lengthy property negotiations is undesirable. The preparation and execution of such endeavors are time-consuming and resource-draining. Constructing the necessary infrastructure and defenses for a property deal can be a lengthy process, ultimately yielding unsatisfactory results.

- Engaging in prolonged property negotiations, akin to besieging a well-fortified city, often leads to frustration and significant resource depletion without achieving the desired outcome. This can result in substantial losses and a weakened position in the market.

- Therefore, a skilled real estate professional seeks to secure property opportunities without protracted negotiations or resource-intensive endeavors. They aim to overcome challenges strategically, without depleting their own resources or resorting to extended disputes.

- By maintaining their resources and strategic advantages intact, a skilled real estate agent can dominate the market without losing a single opportunity. This method is akin to the art of attacking through strategic planning rather than brute force.

- In real estate, the tactical approach varies according to the circumstances. When your resources significantly outnumber those of your competitors, you can strategically encircle them. If your resources are superior but not overwhelming, it may be wise to divide your efforts.

- When the resources are balanced, engaging in direct competition is an option, but when you are at a disadvantage, it may be prudent to withdraw from the market.

- While a smaller real estate force may put up a fierce struggle, it is typically the larger force that prevails in the end.

- In real estate, the agent serves as the protector of their client's interests. A competent and well-prepared agent is the key to a successful property transaction. A deficiency in this regard weakens the client's position.

- There are three ways in which a real estate agent can jeopardize their client's interests:

  (1) By issuing commands without understanding the complexities of a transaction, leading to unrealistic expectations.

  (2) By attempting to manage real estate deals in the same manner as governing a kingdom, disregarding the unique dynamics of property transactions.

  (3) By selecting agents and professionals without considering their suitability for the specific circumstances, undermining the client's confidence.

- When a real estate agent is restless, ill-prepared, or loses the trust of their clients, it invites competition from other agents and agencies, potentially leading to chaos in the market.

- Success in real estate hinges on five essential

principles:

(1) Knowing when to engage and when to abstain from property transactions.

(2) Skillfully managing both superior and inferior property deals.

(3) Fostering a unified purpose and spirit among all participants in a real estate transaction.

(4) Preparing oneself for opportunities and seizing them when the competition is unprepared.

(5) Possessing real estate expertise and autonomy, free from interference.

- The wisdom of real estate lies in understanding these five principles. As the saying goes, "If you know the market and understand your client's needs, you need not fear any challenge. If you know the market but not your client, success and failure may be equally likely. However, if you are ignorant of both the market and your client, you will face difficulties in every transaction."

Chapter 5

Tactical Dispositions

- In the realm of real estate, the art of success involves strategies that mirror the wisdom of ancient fighters who positioned themselves beyond the realm of defeat, patiently awaiting the opportune moment to prevail.

- The most skilled real estate professionals first secure themselves against the possibility of failure and then patiently await the perfect circumstances for success.

- Protecting oneself from failure in real estate is within one's control, but seizing the opportunity to triumph is often dependent on external factors, such as market conditions and client decisions.

- A proficient real estate agent can safeguard their interests, but they cannot always guarantee victory in every transaction.

- It is said that one may understand how to achieve victory without necessarily having the capability to accomplish it.

- Ensuring security against defeat often involves defensive strategies in real estate, while defeating the competition requires taking the initiative and being offensive.

- Defending one's position in real estate suggests a lack of strength or resources, while going on the offensive implies an abundance of resources and a proactive stance.

- A real estate professional skilled in defense operates discreetly and cautiously, while an expert in offense seizes opportunities boldly and decisively. This duality allows for both self-preservation and triumph.

- True excellence in real estate is not merely achieving victory when it is apparent to all but understanding when to act before the common crowd recognizes the opportunity.

- Likewise, it is not the pinnacle of success for a real estate agent to win and receive accolades from the entire industry.

- Small feats do not necessarily demonstrate great competence in real estate, just as merely observing the basics does not signify exceptional insight or hearing thunder does not indicate acute hearing.

- The true master in real estate is one who not only achieves victory but does so effortlessly, without errors or complications.

- Such a real estate professional may not gain a reputation for wisdom or courage, as their victories are achieved without fanfare.

- Victory in real estate is built on a foundation of avoiding mistakes, ensuring that victory is already assured by the time the battle commences.

- A skillful real estate strategist positions themselves in a way that makes defeat impossible, and they seize the moment for victory with precision.

- In real estate, a victorious strategist seeks the battle only after securing victory, whereas one destined for defeat often rushes into battle before considering the outcome.

- The consummate real estate leader adheres to ethical principles, methodical approaches, and disciplined strategies. Through these means, they gain control over their own success.

- In the realm of real estate strategy, there are five key elements: measurement, estimation of quantity, calculation, balancing of chances, and victory.

- Measurement in real estate is akin to assessing the lay of the land, estimation of quantity involves gauging the value of properties, calculation pertains to financial planning, balancing of chances considers risk and reward, and victory is the ultimate goal.

- In real estate, a triumphant agent facing a vanquished competitor is as a pound's weight against a single grain.

- The force of a successful real estate professional entering the market is akin to the release of pent-up waters cascading into a profound chasm. Such is the essence of tactical prowess in real estate.

Chapter 6

Energy

- In the arena of real estate, the principles of control and strategy, whether with a large or small clientele, are guided by similar principles as in warfare. Effective real estate professionals employ tactics that ensure their clients' interests are well-served and secure, employing both direct and indirect methods.

- Managing a substantial real estate portfolio employs the same principles as handling a modest one; it's about effective organization and resource allocation.

- Successfully navigating real estate transactions with a large client base requires clear communication through signs and signals, just as it does with a smaller clientele.

- In real estate, ensuring the stability of your portfolio in the face of market challenges involves both direct and indirect strategies.

- To make your real estate endeavors resilient, like a grindstone striking an egg without breaking it, requires a keen understanding of strengths and weaknesses in property investments.

- In real estate, while direct methods are useful for initiating transactions, achieving victory often demands indirect strategies.

- The application of indirect real estate tactics is as vast and adaptable as the natural world, with the potential to bring forth new opportunities and solutions, much like the eternal cycles of nature.

- Although there are just five musical notes, countless melodies emerge from their combinations.

- Similarly, there are only five primary colors, but their combinations produce a multitude of shades and hues.

- Likewise, five cardinal tastes can yield a wide

array of flavors when combined creatively.

- In the real estate realm, there are primarily two approaches—direct and indirect tactics, yet their combinations give rise to an endless array of strategies.

- Direct and indirect tactics in real estate are interconnected and can be applied in a continuous cycle, akin to moving in a circle without a definitive end.

- The momentum of a real estate transaction can resemble the rush of a torrent, even moving seemingly immovable obstacles.

- Effective decision-making in real estate is akin

to the precise swoop of a falcon, allowing for swift and accurate actions.

- A skilled real estate professional should be formidable in their approach and decisive in their actions.

- Energy in real estate is like drawing a crossbow; decision-making is akin to releasing the trigger.

- Amid the complexity of real estate negotiations, apparent disorder may exist, but it does not equate to true chaos. A well-structured strategy can withstand challenges.

- Simulated disorder in real estate implies a

high degree of underlying discipline, feigned fear assumes inner courage, and apparent weakness masks actual strength.

- Concealing order within apparent disorder involves strategic organization, hiding courage behind timidity relies on reserved energy, and masking strength with weakness can be achieved through tactical maneuvering.

- A skillful real estate agent keeps the competition guessing by creating deceptive appearances, leading competitors to make decisions that benefit the strategist's objectives. They use bait to keep the competition engaged.

- By presenting opportunities, they entice the competition to act, while lying in wait with a carefully selected team to capitalize on the situation.

- The adept real estate strategist harnesses the combined energy of their team, understanding that success relies on the collective effort rather than individual performance.

- When coordinated effectively, the real estate team becomes like rolling logs or stones, with the ability to adapt to different situations.

- The energy harnessed by skilled real estate professionals is comparable to the momentum of a round stone rolling down a mountainside, demonstrating the potential for immense impact.

Chapter 7

Weak Points and Strong

- In the real estate field, as in war, the first to take initiative and be prepared will enter the market with vigor, while those who lag behind will find themselves exhausted.

- Hence, a savvy real estate professional asserts their strategies and goals on the market, rather than allowing the market to dictate their actions.

- By offering attractive opportunities, a real estate agent can entice potential clients to approach willingly. Conversely, by exposing market flaws, they can dissuade unfavorable transactions.

- When the real estate market is at ease, opportunities can be seized. When supply is abundant, demand can be cultivated. In tranquil market conditions, urgency can be created.

- Real estate professionals should position themselves strategically in locations that demand attention, responding quickly to emerging opportunities.

- Real estate ventures can cover extensive distances smoothly when they navigate through untapped markets.

- Success in real estate comes by attacking the markets where competitors are absent and securing positions that are impervious to attack.

- A shrewd real estate agent excels in attacking the market's weak points and defending their clients against potential threats.

- The art of subtlety and secrecy in real estate empowers us to control the outcome of transactions, preserving our clients' interests.

- By targeting the market's vulnerabilities, a

real estate professional can advance confidently, knowing they can outmaneuver their competition.

- If we seek to engage with a client who is currently sheltered from our influence, we can divert our efforts elsewhere to compel them to respond.

- When we aim to avoid conflict, we can take actions that create confusion and uncertainty for potential competitors.

- By understanding market conditions and remaining discreet in our actions, we can focus our efforts while our competitors are divided.

- Unity within our real estate team contrasts with the fragmented approach of our competitors, providing us with a numerical advantage.

- Attacking a market with a superior force against an inferior one positions us for success in real estate.

- Keeping the location and timing of our real estate endeavors concealed forces our competitors to spread their resources thinly.

- Our adversaries' attempts to strengthen their positions in different areas create opportunities for us to exploit their weaknesses.

- Numerical superiority results from compelling our competitors to make extensive preparations, while we remain agile.

- Knowing the time and place of real estate battles allows us to focus our efforts efficiently.

- In the absence of such knowledge, being separated by even a small distance can hamper our ability to support one another effectively.

- Even when faced with a larger number of properties, superior strategy can lead to victory in real estate.

- By preventing our competitors from taking action, we gain the upper hand in real estate negotiations.

- Gathering intelligence about the market and understanding the psychology of our competitors allows us to identify vulnerabilities.

- A careful comparison of our real estate resources with those of our competitors guides our strategy.

- In real estate, as in war, the highest level of tactics is to conceal them, making us immune to the scrutiny of rivals.

- Achieving victory through our opponent's tactics is a concept that eludes most, but it is the essence of true strategic mastery.

- Everyone can see the tactics by which I win real estate transactions, but what remains hidden is the overarching strategy that leads to victory.

- Replicating the same approach that led to one real estate success is not always effective; adaptability is key.

- Real estate tactics, like water, follow the path of least resistance and seek out opportunities.

- In real estate, it is wise to avoid strong competition and focus on opportunities where there is less resistance.

- Just as water adapts its course to the terrain, a real estate professional must adjust their approach to suit the market conditions they face.

- Real estate, like water, is subject to constant change, with no fixed conditions.

- A real estate agent who can adjust their strategies to their competition and the evolving market is truly exceptional.

- The real estate market, like nature's elements and seasons, is subject to continuous transformation and variation.

Chapter 8

Maneuvering

- In real estate, the agent receives their instructions from the client.

- After assembling a portfolio of properties and organizing their resources, a real estate agent must integrate and coordinate various elements before proceeding with their transactions.

- Following that, comes strategic maneuvering, which is often a challenging task. The difficulty in strategic maneuvering lies in transforming complexity into simplicity and turning adversity into opportunity.

- To adopt a long and circuitous route, lure potential buyers away from it, and still reach the goal before them demonstrates mastery of the art of diversion.

- Strategizing in real estate is advantageous when dealing with an organized market but perilous when dealing with a disorganized one.

- If you mobilize a fully prepared real estate team to seize an opportunity, you may find yourself too late. Conversely, detaching a specialized team for the task may involve sacrificing resources.

- Therefore, if you instruct your agents to act swiftly without rest, covering double the usual ground to secure an advantage, the leaders of your divisions may lose their effectiveness.

- The stronger agents will lead, while the less motivated ones will lag behind, and in this manner, only a fraction of your real estate team will succeed.

- If you pursue a strategy of rapid action to outmaneuver the competition, you risk losing your top agents and only a portion of your team will achieve success.

- If you act swiftly and decisively in real estate, you may lose critical team members in the process.

- In real estate, you must understand your neighbors' intentions before considering alliances.

- Navigating the real estate landscape effectively requires knowledge of the local geography, including property features, challenges, and opportunities.

- Before engaging in real estate transactions, having local expertise is essential to understanding market dynamics.

- Real estate professionals should utilize local knowledge to gain a competitive edge.

- In real estate negotiations, employ discretion and strategic positioning to achieve success, moving only when advantageous.

- Whether to concentrate or diversify real estate efforts depends on the specific circumstances.

- Real estate strategies should balance rapidity, like the wind, with stability, like a forest.

- In real estate, when choosing between action and inaction, adapt your approach to the situation.

- Conceal your plans in real estate transactions and move decisively when the time is right.

- When engaging in real estate ventures, ensure that the spoils are distributed fairly among your team members.

- Contemplate and deliberate before taking action in the real estate market.

- Success in real estate lies in mastering the art of diversion.

- In real estate, employ various means, such as marketing and communication tools, to capture the attention of potential clients and competitors.

- Visual and auditory cues, like marketing materials and presentations, are essential in real estate to engage with clients effectively.

- In real estate, using visual and auditory cues helps align clients' focus and attention.

- By creating a cohesive and synchronized real estate team, it is possible to ensure that both the fearless and hesitant are aligned in their actions.

- The spirit of a real estate team can be influenced, and a leader's clarity of mind can be compromised.

- A real estate agent should recognize that motivation is highest in the morning, decreases by noon, and dwindles by evening.

- A wise real estate agent avoids competing with an energized market but seizes opportunities when it becomes more passive.

- In real estate, maintaining composure and observing the market's mood is essential.

- A disciplined real estate agent knows when to act decisively and when to wait for opportunities.

- In real estate, understanding market conditions and timing is crucial.

- Avoid uphill battles in real estate and choose the right circumstances to engage with clients.

- Do not pursue clients who pretend to lose interest, and do not challenge motivated buyers.

- In real estate, do not fall for tempting offers from competitors, and avoid intervening when clients are satisfied with their decisions.

- When presenting real estate opportunities, leave room for clients to explore alternatives, and do not press too hard when dealing with reluctant buyers.

- Such is the art of real estate.

Chapter 9

Variation of Tactics

- In real estate, the agent receives their instructions from the client, compiles property listings, and organizes resources.

- When dealing with challenging property situations, avoid idling. In areas with intersecting markets, collaborate with fellow professionals. Refrain from isolating yourself in risky locations. In difficult circumstances, strategize; in desperate cases, take action.

- There are properties that shouldn't be pursued, clients that shouldn't be engaged, listings that shouldn't be marketed, deals that shouldn't be contested, and client demands that shouldn't be met.

- The real estate agent who comprehends the benefits of adapting strategies can effectively navigate the market.

- However, a real estate agent who lacks this understanding, even with ample market knowledge, may struggle to apply their expertise.

- Thus, a real estate professional who doesn't adapt their strategies, even with knowledge of market dynamics, may not maximize their potential.

- In successful real estate plans, both advantages and disadvantages should be considered.

- By tempering our expectations of advantage, we can achieve the core of our objectives.

- When faced with difficulties, being ready to seize opportunities can help overcome adversity.

- Disrupt competitors by causing them damage and creating distractions. Attract them to specific properties or areas.

- In real estate, anticipate the client's actions and be prepared, focusing on making your services indispensable.

- There are five critical mistakes that can affect a real estate agent: (1) Being too reckless, leading to failure; (2) cowardice, resulting in missed opportunities; (3) impulsive reactions to insults; (4) sensitivity to reputation; (5) excessive worry about clients' concerns.

- These are the five common pitfalls in real estate, detrimental to a successful career.

- When a real estate deal fails and your reputation is damaged, these five mistakes are likely the root causes. Reflect on them.

THE ART OF REAL ESTATE

Chapter 10

The Army On The March

- In real estate, finding suitable locations and observing market indicators is crucial. Move swiftly over different areas, and stay informed about trends.

- Seek properties in high-demand areas with good exposure to sunlight. Avoid purchasing properties in challenging locations solely for the purpose of selling them later.

- After completing a transaction in one market, diversify your investments.

- When facing competition in the real estate market, don't rush to confront it head-on. Instead, wait for the right opportunity.

- If you are eager to make a deal, don't confront a competing buyer or seller directly, especially near a transaction point.

- Position your properties higher in value and exposure than the competition, and avoid competing in areas where demand is low.

- When dealing with distressed properties, act

quickly to minimize risks.

- In case you need to negotiate a deal involving a distressed property, ensure access to necessary resources and position the property favorably.

- In dry, competitive markets, focus on easy-to-access properties in safe locations with potential for value appreciation.

- These principles are essential for real estate success, as demonstrated by those who have excelled in the industry.

- High-quality properties tend to be more attractive and valuable.

- The right approach to property management can prevent issues and lead to victory.

- When choosing a location, consider the orientation and surroundings to maximize property appeal.

- In case of adverse weather conditions, wait until the situation improves before proceeding with your real estate plans.

- Avoid properties in challenging environments, such as those with steep terrain or dense vegetation.

- While you avoid such locations, use them

strategically to your advantage.

- Carefully inspect and search properties in areas with natural obstacles and hidden potential risks.

- When your competitors are positioned to your advantage, consider their tactics.

- When your competition encourages you to advance, proceed with caution.

- If the market appears too accessible, exercise caution, as it may be an attempt to lure you in.

- Monitor the movement and behavior of your peers in the real estate industry.

- Observe how others adapt to changing market conditions.

- When you encounter obstacles, stay the course and maintain your position.

- When the market is uncertain, be cautious and consider alternatives.

- Make use of high-quality resources, both natural and artificial, to enhance property value.

- Evaluate negotiations carefully and insist on

commitments.

- Address problems proactively and handle challenges as they arise.

- Maintain discipline within your team and respond to changing circumstances.

- Manage your resources effectively, ensuring they're used efficiently.

- Act swiftly to address any issues that may hinder progress.

- When your team is exhausted, provide necessary support.

- Keep an eye on potential threats to your real estate investments.

- Adapt to changing market conditions, staying prepared for sudden shifts.

- Keep communication lines open and address any unrest among team members.

- Recognize signs of discontent among your colleagues.

- Avoid excessive rewards and punishments.

- Be consistent in your approach and avoid

overconfidence.

- Use diplomacy when necessary, but remain cautious.

- When the situation is tense, maintain vigilance and awareness.

- In the face of an evenly matched competition, focus on strategy, vigilance, and reinforcements.

- Display confidence but remain cautious.

- Maintain a balance between discipline and empathy when dealing with team members.

- Discipline is key to success in real estate.

- Enforce rules consistently to maintain discipline.

- Combine confidence in your team with the insistence on following your strategies for mutual success.

Chapter 11

Terrain

- In real estate, different types of properties and market conditions can be compared to various terrains: (1) accessible properties; (2) challenging properties; (3) uncertain properties; (4) properties with limited potential; (5) highly desirable properties; (6) properties in distant locations.

- "Accessible" properties are those that are easy to buy and sell. When dealing with accessible properties, try to secure desirable locations with good visibility and protect your investment by ensuring a stable stream of income. This approach can give you a competitive advantage.

- "Challenging" properties may be difficult to acquire and may not provide immediate returns. When dealing with challenging properties, assess the risks carefully. If the opportunity arises, consider making a move, but be cautious about overcommitting, as failure can lead to significant losses.

- "Uncertain" properties are those where it is difficult to predict market trends. In such cases, it may be wise to observe the market rather than taking immediate action. Wait for the right time to invest and capitalize on opportunities when they arise.

- "Properties with limited potential" may not offer significant returns on investment. When dealing with such properties, avoid competing aggressively for them. Instead, consider alternative opportunities that may provide better returns.

- "Highly desirable" properties are in great demand. When dealing with these properties, act quickly to secure them and gain an advantage over competitors.

- To avoid overcommitting to properties in "distant locations," carefully evaluate whether the benefits outweigh the challenges. Be prepared to adapt your strategy and consider other options if necessary.

- Just as an army faces six calamities, real estate investors may encounter challenges in their investments. These include (1) financial loss; (2) management issues; (3) property value depreciation; (4) foreclosure or insolvency; (5) organizational problems; (6) catastrophic investment failure.

- Real estate investors must be prepared for these challenges, which can result from poor decisions or mismanagement.

- Recognize that the outcome of an investment is not solely determined by the size of the investment but by careful planning and execution.

- When common investors are not adequately

informed and are financially unprepared, it can lead to financial loss.

- Effective management and strong leadership are essential for successful real estate investments.

- In cases where property management is ineffective or the roles of team members are unclear, investments may depreciate in value.

- Effective organization and planning are crucial for managing real estate investments.

- When a property investment is not well-planned or is rushed, it may result in a catastrophic failure.

- Investors must carefully assess their situations and adapt their strategies accordingly to achieve success.

- The natural state of the real estate market can be an investor's greatest ally. However, understanding the market, controlling variables, and making informed decisions are essential for success.

- Investors who have a deep understanding of the market and make informed decisions are more likely to succeed.

- Invest based on facts, not emotions. Make calculated decisions that align with your investment goals.

- Sometimes, taking action is necessary, even if it means going against conventional wisdom or advice. However, always evaluate the risks and benefits before making a decision.

- A responsible real estate investor focuses on protecting their investments and serving the best interests of their clients and stakeholders.

- Building strong relationships with your team members can foster loyalty and dedication.

- Invest time and effort in building trust and maintaining strong relationships with your team.

- Gain the loyalty of your team members by treating them like family.

- If your team is dedicated to your goals and objectives, they will support you in challenging times.

- A disciplined approach to leadership and investment management is essential for success.

- Maintain discipline and a clear sense of purpose in your real estate investments.

- Enforce your investment strategies consistently to ensure disciplined decision-making.

- Keep a watchful eye on market conditions and your own readiness for investment opportunities.

- Plan your investments carefully and adapt your strategies as needed.

- Real estate investors must balance market dynamics, property characteristics, and financial considerations to achieve success.

- Thoroughly understand market conditions, property features, and financial aspects to make informed investment decisions.

- Make investment choices that align with your

goals, even if it means avoiding certain opportunities.

- Know when to take action and when to exercise restraint.

- Be aware of your own capabilities and limitations and communicate effectively with your team.

- Avoid making hasty decisions without considering all relevant factors.

- Adapt to changing market conditions and make informed choices that benefit your investments.

- Maintain your authority as a leader and enforce your strategies consistently.

- Address issues and challenges as they arise to maintain control over your investments.

- Avoid overcommitting to investments when the situation is unfavorable, and be prepared to adjust your strategies.

- Confidence and a clear sense of purpose are essential for leadership and successful real estate investing.

- Maintain a balance between being a compassionate leader and enforcing your investment strategies.

- Discipline is key to achieving success in the real estate market.

- Consistently enforce your investment strategies to maintain discipline in your investments.

- Leadership and decision-making skills, combined with discipline and adaptability, are crucial for achieving success in real estate investing.

Chapter 12

The Nine Situations

Sun Tzu describes nine types of terrain that are relevant in warfare. These terrains have different strategic implications for conducting and winning battles. In the context of real estate, these principles can be adapted to understand various market conditions and scenarios that real estate professionals might encounter. Here's how each type of ground can be reinterpreted:

1. **Dispersive Ground**: This represents a real estate market where an agent is operating within their familiar territory or comfort

zone. Just as a chieftain in their own territory must be wary of becoming complacent, agents should avoid becoming too comfortable and neglecting their professional development or market research.

2. **Facile Ground**: When a real estate agent ventures slightly beyond their familiar territory, such as into a nearby or similar market, they must be cautious and not overextend themselves. This is similar to a commander who has entered enemy territory but not too deeply.

3. **Contentious Ground**: This type of ground in real estate refers to highly competitive markets, where significant advantages can be gained or lost. Agents must be strategic in such markets, understanding the high stakes and intense competition.

4. **Open Ground**: A market where movement and opportunities are plentiful for all agents,

similar to terrain that offers freedom of movement for all armies.

5. **Ground of Intersecting Highways**: This represents key strategic markets or hubs that offer significant advantages due to their connectivity and high demand. Controlling such a market can give an agent a considerable advantage.

6. **Serious Ground**: This is akin to an agent deeply committed to a market far from their base of operations, where withdrawal would be difficult. Such situations require full commitment and careful planning.

7. **Difficult Ground**: Markets that are challenging to operate in due to various factors like low demand, high uncertainty, or economic instability are like difficult terrains in warfare.

8. **Hemmed-In Ground**: Situations where an

agent is in a market that offers limited options or ways out, requiring innovative strategies and possibly alliances for survival and success.

9. **Desperate Ground**: A scenario where an agent's survival in the market is at risk, requiring them to fight hard and innovate to stay afloat.

In adapting Sun Tzu's principles to real estate, it's crucial to recognize the strategic importance of understanding your market environment, just as a general must understand the terrain to be successful in battle.

Strategic Disruption: Just as ancient leaders disrupted the enemy's coordination, real estate professionals should aim to disrupt the market competition by creating unique value propositions. This might involve innovative marketing strategies, unique service offerings, or leveraging technology to differentiate their services from the competition. The goal is to prevent competitors from forming a unified front and to keep them off balance.

Opportunistic Action: This speaks to the importance of timing in real estate. A skilled agent recognizes the right moment to make a move, whether it's listing a property, making an offer, or entering a new market. They understand when to act aggressively and when to hold back, always with an eye on leveraging the most advantageous timing.

Leveraging Key Assets: In real estate, this could mean identifying and securing a property or asset that is highly valued in the market. This could be a property in a high-demand area or one with unique features. Securing such assets can give real estate professionals leverage in negotiations and influence in the market.

Speed and Surprise: Rapid response to market changes and the ability to capitalize on unexpected opportunities can give real estate agents a significant advantage. This might involve quickly adapting to new market trends or being the first to adopt new technologies or marketing strategies.

Deep Market Penetration: The deeper a real estate professional penetrates into a specific market segment, the more they understand it and the stronger their position becomes. This can involve specializing in a particular type of property or a specific geographic area.

Team Management and Planning: Care for the well-being of your team and avoid overworking them. Maintain high morale and ensure that energy and resources are used efficiently. Continuous learning and strategic planning are essential.

Resilience in Adversity: In challenging market conditions, the most resilient agents, who are willing to face difficulties head-on, often emerge successful. This involves maintaining a strong, positive attitude and being prepared to tackle tough situations.

Team Independence and Initiative: Encourage a team culture where members are proactive, take the initiative, and are reliable without constant supervision. This independence can lead to more innovative and effective approaches to selling real estate.

Rational Decision-Making: Emphasize the importance of making decisions based on data and rational analysis, rather than superstition or emotion. This approach reduces the risk of making poor decisions in high-pressure situations.

Flexibility and Adaptability: A skilled real estate tactician is adaptable and can respond effectively to attacks from any direction. This means being prepared to adjust strategies quickly in response to changes in the market or actions by competitors.

Adaptability and Teamwork: In real estate, like in warfare, adaptability and the ability to work effectively under varying circumstances are crucial. Real estate agents must collaborate, sometimes even with competitors, in situations like joint ventures or co-listings, much like enemies who cooperate in a storm.

Beyond Conventional Trust: Trust in real estate should not be solely based on traditional methods or assumptions. It's important to verify information and stay vigilant, similar to not just relying on tethering horses or burying chariot wheels for security.

Standard of Excellence: Set a high standard of professionalism and ethics in your real estate practice. This standard should be uniform across your team, ensuring consistency in service and reputation.

Leveraging Strengths and Weaknesses: Understand the strengths and weaknesses of your team and the market. Use this knowledge to position your real estate business effectively, whether in a buyer's or seller's market, or in different property segments.

Unified Leadership: Lead your real estate team with a clear vision, guiding them through complex transactions and market shifts as if you were leading a single person.

Discretion and Order: Maintain confidentiality in client dealings and be organized in your approach. This ensures trust and respect from clients and colleagues.

Strategic Misdirection: In negotiations or competitive situations, it can be effective to use misdirection to protect client interests or to gain a more favorable position.

Flexibility in Strategy: Be ready to change your real estate strategies in response to market changes, keeping competitors and market forces uncertain of your next move.

Decisive Action: In critical situations, such as bidding wars or unique market opportunities, act decisively and commit fully to your strategy.

Total Commitment: Demonstrate total commitment to your real estate objectives, leaving no room for hesitation.

Understanding the Market: Deeply understand the various conditions of the real estate market, analogous to a general understanding different terrains, and adapt your tactics accordingly.

Deep Market Engagement: Engage deeply with the real estate market you are operating in. Understand the nuances and leverage your position, whether you are a local expert or entering new markets.

Tactics for Different Market Conditions: Develop specific tactics for different types of markets (e.g., buyer's market, seller's market, balanced market) and be prepared for challenging situations.

Local Knowledge and Alliances: Utilize local market knowledge and build alliances with other real estate professionals, such as mortgage brokers, home inspectors, and lawyers.

Comprehensive Strategy and Execution: Have a comprehensive understanding of the real estate industry and execute your strategies with precision, foresight, and adaptability.

Strategic Patience and Swift Action: Be patient and wait for the right opportunity in the market, but once it presents itself, act swiftly and decisively.

Chapter 13

The Attack By Fire

Diverse Strategies for Market Dominance: Just as there are five ways of attacking with fire in warfare, real estate professionals can employ multiple strategies to dominate the market. These could include aggressive marketing campaigns, leveraging new technology, innovative financing options, or providing exceptional customer service to outperform competitors.

Responsive and Proactive Tactics: Be prepared to respond quickly to market changes (e.g., policy changes, economic shifts) and take proactive steps at the right moment. For instance, adapting to a market downturn by focusing on rentals or seizing an opportunity in a booming market segment.

Timing and Persistence: Understand that market conditions can change rapidly. Being able to adapt to these changes and persist through challenging periods is crucial in real estate.

Intelligence and Strength: Use market intelligence and robust networks as aids in your real estate business. This involves staying informed about market trends and maintaining strong relationships with clients and other stakeholders.

Limiting Competition Without Total Elimination: In real estate negotiations or when dealing with competitors, sometimes the goal is not to completely outdo the competition but to gain a strategic advantage.

Enterprise and Planning: Cultivating a spirit of enterprise and thorough planning is essential in real estate. This could involve exploring new markets, continuous learning, and strategic planning for long-term success.

Calculated Moves: Make moves in the real estate market only when there is a clear advantage or benefit. This could involve buying or selling properties, expanding into new areas, or investing in new technologies.

Emotional Intelligence and Long-Term Perspective: Maintain a balanced perspective and avoid making decisions based on transient emotions. Understand that some losses or setbacks are irreversible, emphasizing the need for careful decision-making.

Caution and Strategy: An effective real estate professional, like a good general, is always cautious and strategic, ensuring sustainable growth and stability in their business.

These strategies highlight the importance of adaptability, intelligence, and strategic planning in real estate. Understanding the market, responding appropriately to different situations, and maintaining a long-term perspective are key to achieving success in the industry.

Chapter 14

The Use of Spies

Resource Management: Just as leading a large army over great distances is costly and taxing, undertaking large-scale real estate projects or expanding into new markets requires significant resources and can have far-reaching impacts. It's important to manage these resources wisely to avoid overextension.

Efficient Use of Information: In real estate, having timely and accurate market information can be the key to securing a deal or making a profitable investment. Skimping on investing in quality market research or expert advice can lead to missed opportunities or financial losses.

Value of Foreknowledge: Just as foreknowledge is critical in warfare, in real estate, understanding market trends, client needs, and competitor strategies ahead of time is invaluable. This knowledge enables better decision-making and strategic planning.

Market Intelligence Sources: Real estate professionals must gather intelligence from various sources, including market reports, local experts, and direct observations. This comprehensive understanding of the market helps in making informed decisions.

Strategic Information Gathering: In real estate, this could be likened to understanding the different stakeholders in the market - from buyers, sellers, other agents, to market analysts. Gathering diverse perspectives can provide a more complete picture of the market dynamics.

Importance of Confidentiality and Strategy: Maintain confidentiality in dealings and use strategic information wisely. This includes being discreet with client information and using market insights to guide business strategies.

Dealing with Competition: In competitive bidding situations or market analysis, understanding the tactics and strategies of other real estate agents can provide a strategic advantage.

Utilizing Information for Strategic Advantage: Use the information gathered to make strategic decisions, such as when to list a property, price a home, or enter a new market segment.

Prioritizing Knowledge Acquisition: Just as the converted spy is crucial in warfare, in real estate, understanding the market and your competition is key to success. This requires continuous learning and staying updated with the latest market trends.

Leveraging Intelligence for Growth: Historical examples in "The Art of War" show the importance of intelligence in the rise of dynasties. Similarly, in real estate, those who use market intelligence effectively are often more successful in their ventures.

These principles underscore the importance of intelligence, strategic planning, and efficient resource management in the real estate industry. They highlight the need for real estate professionals to be well-informed, adaptable, and strategic in their operations.

www.ingramcontent.com/pod-product-compliance
Lightning Source LLC
Chambersburg PA
CBHW060818050426
42449CB00008B/1713